SIGNS OF MARRIAGE:
POEMS

poems by

Carla Schwartz

Finishing Line Press
Georgetown, Kentucky

SIGNS OF MARRIAGE:
POEMS

Copyright © 2022 by Carla Schwartz
ISBN 978-1-64662-857-5 First Edition
All rights reserved under International and Pan-American Copyright Conventions. No part of this book may be reproduced in any manner whatsoever without written permission from the publisher, except in the case of brief quotations embodied in critical articles and reviews.

ACKNOWLEDGMENTS

The author is also grateful to the editors of the following publications for publishing previous versions of some of the poems in this collection.

"2020: Were you to have Lived," Mayor of Boston's Arts and Culture Poetry Program, 2022
"Contemplating Humanity While Swimming," *Eastern Iowa Review*, Issue 12, 2020,
"Dagobert Peche," *Discretionary Love*, 2021
"Equinox Sunset," *Poetry Quarterly*, Fall, 2021
"Farm Life," *Leon Literary Review* #14, 2022
"Father on his Driveway," T*he MacGuffin*, 2022
"For What Gnaws at You," *Sport Literate*, 2020
"It Wasn't the Gun," *Discretionary Love*, 2021
"On Seeking Forgiveness, After Simic," *Triggerfish Critical Review*, December 2017
"Promise" *Poetorium Father's Day 2021 Anthology*, 2021
"Sweet Potato Harvest," *Tales from the Forest*, May 2018
"Turntable Park," *Ibbetson Street*, Winter 2021
"This rope," *Lost River Literary Magazine*, Summer 2018
"Voodoo," *Misfit Magazine*, Fall/Winter 2020
"Your Table Saw," *Misfit Magazine*, Fall/Winter 2020
"Weighing a December Swim," *Lost River Review*, Summer 2018

Publisher: Leah Huete de Maines
Editor: Christen Kincaid
Cover Art: Carla Schwartz
Author Photo: Marietta Hitzemann
Cover Design: Elizabeth Maines McCleavy

Order online: www.finishinglinepress.com
also available on amazon.com

Author inquiries and mail orders:
Finishing Line Press
PO Box 1626
Georgetown, Kentucky 40324
USA

Table of Contents

Stones 1
Love Poem, ... 2
Skating Black Ice 3
Love Is Like Dredging 4
Marriage, Two Signs 5
2020: Were You to Have Lived 7
Houseboating 9
Promise 10
Love-Struck 11
Raspberries 12
Farm Life 13
On Seeking Forgiveness, After Simic 14
Turntable Park 15
This Rope 16
It Wasn't The Gun 17
Your Table Saw 19
Dagobert Peche 20
For What Gnaws at You 21
Antique Lamp 22
River 23
Contemplating Humanity While Swimming 24
Weighing a December Swim 25
Equinox Sunset 26
Sweet Potato Harvest 27
Father On His Driveway 28
First Shots 30
Dedication 32
Voodoo 33
Leonard Cohen Argues 34

Dedicated to the memory of my parents, who hung in there through thick and thin for 55 years, and to Claude, who knows where the stones belong.

Stones

You began with just one rock mid-puddle of the front yard—
we named it *Rock Hudson*—but then came two more to bookend the
	mud—
Rock-Around-the-Clock and *Elizabeth Taylor*.

I loved the line of them—the symmetry. I never questioned the origins—
you'd just arrive there at our sunken front yard one large rock
in the wheel barrow at a time until this was no random arrangement.

You said you had one rule of rock—*The flat side always goes down*
so that hump-side up a rock might settle into its new home.

Next you made a line of rocks to guide the Y of our two stone paths—
a kind of smile I said—a rock smile—and you smiled and the next day
and the next—two more rocks to make the eyes.

A few weeks later a nose appeared—a little bent
a little sad but a nose.

Then the effort changed—you graduated from pry bar and shovel
to blocks, straps, and a come-along.

Soon you urged thousand-pound boulders to find their new sweet spot
in our yard—most flat-side down—until I told you I liked the flat side

so we pried blocked and tipped together
until one flat face shone back at us.

One morning you brought me to the back yard and showed me
the aisle you had created with the stones you'd moved.

I said *Well, if we ever get married this will be our aisle*
and you rolled your eyes but later handed me something

palm-sized with a planar face—a glittery stone
of mica and quartz.

Love Poem,

as you help me tend this home
be my band saw my flathead my jig
be my calk my foam *(Great Stuff)*
trim out my gaps and seal my sills.

Lend me balance lest I slip
from a ladder or a step
lend me strength to hold and lift
as I sand my ragged edge.

Love poem, tend my seeds
better than I could succeed
bring me brazen shears
that I might snip the fruits you bear

and as time slips through my pen
blow love kisses to the wind.

Skating Black Ice

is even better
after skating bumps

better than walking on ice
hearing it crunch

under the spikes
fixed in my shoes

that propel me
forward—not down—

on black ice
I glide like a sail—

blade   glide
  blade   glide

free to fly
hors d'fear

of falling
of breaking
of crashing through—

better than thinking
better than grieving

better than almost anything
other than you.

Love Is Like Dredging

When you ply your shovel
to the sand at lake bottom—
this shallow lake in drought

you might not hear
the ping as your blade stops
short against stone.

You must not give up
just work around it—
dig beneath until you release

the impediment.
Lift and carry away
the sand, the stones

cupped in your spade.
Hold your arms
level as you

ferry to shore
where I stand and wait
where I stretch out my own arms

to take from you
what you've dredged up
for us both.

Marriage, Two Signs

Driving South on Route 3,
just over the Massachusetts line,
I saw two signs, hand-painted in red—

Drain the Swamp

Probe Obama

The first sign made me think
of our front yard,
in flood this time of year,
deep enough for the Mallard couple
to dive happily, dive and dive,
oblivious to my snapping photos,
and how, before seeing them there,
dining together in marital bliss,
I had contemplated ways I might try
to drain our little swamped lawn—
digging gullies, laying down stones or sand,
but the Mallards seemed to be doing a fine job—
each day, a little less water in the yard—
I didn't want to *drain the swamp* anymore,
rather, I wondered how the ducks would fare
when the yard dried up.

The second sign reminded me of *Becoming*,
Michelle's autobiography,
how she laid out her love for all to read—
poked, prodded, *probed*, even,
so that not only was Michelle likeable,
her sometimes self-centered, nerdish,
cigarette-smoking husband
was likeable, no, loveable, too,
and as a reader, you entered their love,

understood no one else would probe
his almost hairless chest, kiss his lips,
or gyrate hips on the dance floor—
I did not want to *probe Obama*,
that's Michelle's domain,
and I thought, *Probe on, Michelle
Obama. Probe on.*

2020: Were you to have Lived

You would have sat down at the kitchen table
with my father that January night,

might have been the one to cook dinner for him—
maybe a frozen soup—and even though he was not feeling well

he might not have been so indifferent
as to wear his pajamas to dinner.

Together at the table, you would have been there
when his knees folded under as he tried to stand up,

might even have caught him, or you'd have driven him
to the doctor that day, or you'd have had more sense than him

to stop the both of you from driving by then.
You would have had a smart phone

would have taken it in hand
punched up an Uber,

and when my father recovered you'd sit calmly
discussing whom to vote for—Bernie, or Kamala.

When the pandemic shut everything down you would have both worn masks
among strangers maybe taken strolls around the block.

But when you'd learned about George Floyd and Brianna Taylor
you'd remember the Nazi soldiers with their guns bursting into your home,

would have mourned for lives lost, mourned
for being too old to stand and protest.

The two of you would have kept company. You'd have handled the
    technology
ordered meals   played the piano   video chatted with your friends.

But by then you were long dead and when my father's knees
buckled him to the floor

as he lay there unable to rise   he might have looked up—
heard you calling to him until the ambulance came.

Houseboating

Like petticoats, the gray clouds gather,
roll one on another, mount to a tower.
Soon low distant grumbles of thunder
roll one then another. Light flashes
from far reaches come closer
as we pull up anchor and start the motor.

Now the boat bucks side-to-side
with the wind-blown waves rolling, lightning bolts
strike clear down to water—I ask is there a chance
we could falter—of course I know more or less
the answer—if lightning strikes the roof
we fry the solar from the inverter wires

down the charge controller to the battery
and there we'd be together, still floating, wouldn't we?

Promise

A promise of hope to ski with my father
unfulfilled amid the snow and the trees—
a pleasure—the joy he once shared with my mother.

We couldn't do better than Saturday's weather.
The cool sunny day, the light winter breeze,
so I promise to ski with my hopeful father.

I urge him to carry some food and water
and to use his less cumbersome skis
for the pleasure he once shared with my mother.

With pink ribbons tied to his poles—his tethers—
I spot him afar, from hundreds of feet,
a hopeless promise to ski with my father.

His ski pace is a crawl, no faster.
He can no longer kick-glide with ease
to practice his pleasure once shared with my mother.

His unflappable will to ski doesn't dither.
Tumbles and icy spots fail to displease.
He vowed ever after so to ski goes my father
a joy first kindled in him by my mother.

Love-struck

When I locked the car
and set out for that swim
that very warm sunny day
unwittingly I approached
a crucial juncture—
as I walked toward the pond
where I once swam with my father
I met the eyes of love
although these were hard to read
I—unaware—didn't realize
I needed convincing
but with my face open
like a shovel I smiled back
and without thinking dug in.

Raspberries

As a man and a woman meet
in the afternoon—safely distanced
across the raspberry patch—
they pick and taste, melt
berry to tongue, lean in
and stretch to reach
a laden branch
some distance
into the heart
of the stand.
As they pick
they move 'round
and 'round the berries—
a berry dance—
you know how it is
with raspberries—
you must circle
more than once
to find what you've missed
the first go-round.

They speak not
the heaviness
of the years
lost between them
begun around some other patch
of fruit—not of their diaspora—
not their chance reunion. No.
Hell no!
Raspberries!
Only raspberries
I tell you these two—
they swallow
the drupelets
ignore
the scratches
between fingers
they pinch
the flavor.

Farm Life

I've called off the folks who bale their hay—
the grasses—growing in my fields—
that now sway quietly in the wind

I called the hunter, who from the blind
he'd built in my stand of pines
picked off deer in his sights,

to say he'd not be hunting here
anymore. There, look, a doe,
her fawn chewing the raspberries—

plants and all—berries my wife
won prizes with—
I haven't gathered since she's gone

and now can't see well enough
to pick the fruit with these clouds
in my eyes. The sky

has begun to cloud. I had the pool
I used to tend filled in. My wife—
no longer around to swim.

Today the hunter shared his last
venison—he brought it in marinade—
I asked would he also bring

a six pack, no, a case, oh a six.
How much longer will it take
before I empty my fridge—

before I'm done with all this?

On Seeking Forgiveness, After Simic

> *Incurable romantics marrying eternal grumblers.*
>   *—Charles Simic, "Promises of Leniency and Forgiveness"*
> *The more innocent you believe you are, / the harder it'll be for you.*
>   *—Charles Simic, "Calamity Crier"*

It turns out
you're the grumbler
I'm the romantic.
But then I grumble back
defending my innocence
until I find myself
wed to difficulty.

Turntable Park

To return home we go by kayak—
the lake this night
not calm, but stirred up.

Before leaving the dock I turn on the light
at the head of my boat—*for safety* I think—
but underway it blinds me.

Alone in my kayak—ahead of you—
blinded in the white darkness—
I'm afraid a wave might drive my boat into a rock.

When you catch up
you switch off my light
in a frenzied blown-about moment

when we both almost crash into the shore
but then we master the fetch
and head south toward our cove.

Almost home, we look up at the moon,
and agree how lovely it is on the lake.
This day could have been any other

except I said "bike path"—so kayaks,
so what?—the wind, the rain, the waves—
so car, so bikes, stone dust,

and autumn leaves fringing the lakeside trail
we must follow to its finish—*Turntable Park*—
because how could you stop short

of a park named for the mechanism
that turns trains around—a backtracking
that anyone might hope for?

This rope

I hold in tension
at arm's length
swing like a lover
hoping he returns
captured round my arms
my palm curled around a hand
not alone anymore
now I have a post
to steady by
to tie up to
a dour-faced overseer—
the two of us
tied by thick strand
to bring us home
a kind of tango
of wrap and friction
swings the stern back
close in toward the dock
this rope—
whipped at the ends
to keep from fraying
to stay worry—
this flower, bloomed open
bluer than sky.

It Wasn't the Gun

but today I'm thinking about it—your gun—
still packed up and ready to load,
the .22, Smith & Wesson
you bought when we moved to Bear Island.

I remove it from the case I gave you one Christmas—
the case you had taken down that Saturday,
in preparation for the season opening
that week—that saddest Saturday,

before it wasn't just another
shimmering November day on our lake.
Our lake—that's how we'd refer to it those thin months
when most other islanders had closed up

for the season. The gun still smells of oil—
you'd cleaned the scope and barrel,
tucked the ammo away in the zipper pocket
I'd had monogrammed for you—*JAM*.

I was always terrified you'd die by this gun
with your hunting buddy nearby.

I lift out your orange vest and hug myself into it
inhaling as I do but I don't smell you.
I smell only the house you built for us—
my very definition of you.

I cradle the rifle under my arm and aim
at the mounted head of the deer
you'd shot that first hunting year—
I pull back the trigger of the unloaded gun
and snap.

I want to shoot holes through all we did,
to cull sense from the inexplicable—
the crash I thought was our running aground,
how much it hurt to grab our phone
from the slump of you, already gone.

After the accident, your picture—
printed in the paper—side-by-side
with a photo of the driver of the other boat—
your hunting buddy—looking young and happy
with a fish on a hook.

In your photo your wrinkles smile to the sun
but oh, that chiseled chin—
I called you *Apollo* for that jaw—
Apollo, who, like you, healed and sang.

Your Table Saw

The first thing I notice is the blade
protruding like a shark fin
but with teeth and no tongue.
My father had a table saw too.

Seeing yours reminds me
of my father's sharp tongue
which, when I was young, cut like a saw
through the air with each of my missteps—

like when I didn't add the garlic
to the meat sauce that first time—
didn't simmer the sauce
with a low enough flame.

Once when I was a teen
my father grabbed my wrists
and blocked my way
with his force.

My father discouraged me
from studying mathematics
after college—told me
I wasn't smart enough.

Now at 91—too tired to shout—
my father sits to go upstairs—
he switches on the motor and rides
his stair lift up and down.

Outside with your table saw—
working on my cubbies—
you measure and cut the boards
then biscuit and glue them.

Dagobert Peche

That for years I wondered what had become of you—
how you managed, made money,
if you ever married that younger woman,
that so many years passed since our last phone call
when you told me you'd nursed your father
to his death, that Google became a lens
from which I could glean the few pinches
of internet signature you left there—a comment
on a moped site, an arrest in front of your childhood home—
that my sister told me she thought she once saw you
in New York with a little boy who resembled you,
that my childbearing years came and went,
that you visited my dreams more than anyone else—
sometimes in a dance, sometimes an embrace, sometimes to die—
that I lived 23 years in the house I thought would be our home
surrounded by your artifacts—
a picture frame, a camera, a mocha set—
that I managed to build a life in that house beyond our love

until I decided to move and so to unclutter—
that for all the ways I imagined we might have met again,
to see your name in an email
in response to my ad,
claiming with such conviction
that the mocha set was yours—

after all these years how could I have known
that to conjure you I need only have mentioned
Dagobert Peche?

For What Gnaws at You

To step onto your paddleboard
while seated at the dock
set your board parallel to the dock
step down into a crouch
the outside foot followed by the inside
and lift your paddle as you stand up
and stroke. Paddle steady—strong.
Switch sides when you start to veer
off-course. For more power
bend your knees as you stroke.
Take in the sun. Paddle into the wind.
Keep tabs on what comes your way—
boats, loons, waves.

As the wind strengthens
stroke even harder.
Use your whole body. Be in it
until the waves win and turn your board
around. Bend your knees
stand your paddle to the waves
surf your way back.

Does your bad day still trouble you?

Antique Lamp

Every once in a while
walking through the garage
I notice the iron lamp
still in need of rewiring
standing in the corner
tall and lanky as you were
a project you left me
all those years ago
along with a couple
of speakers—once very fine
but ready to bust so I wonder—
if I make the repairs
would I miss you more
or less?

River

We take the path   along the Charles
maybe to kill time   we think   but
time is all we have   as we walk
along the path   as the blackbirds
flit from branch to branch   and sing
to us   when we notice the ducks
Mallards   male and female   mating
at the river bank as if   the sole
two survivors on this earth   splashing
swishing but then a muskrat swims by
with all he has paddling his little paws
not stopping   to watch   the ducks
but diving   every so often   diving
checking roots   looking for home.

Contemplating Humanity While Swimming

After a mile I stop paddling and drift.
I strap an orange swim buoy around my waist
and then don the goggles, gloves, fins.

Like a mink on a rock, I slip off my board—
I begin arm over arm on my back
towing the board behind me.

The wind tickles the water's surface.
In the cool air I can't help wonder
if there is snow on top of Mount Washington.

Alan's admonishment gnaws at me:
You can't write a poem that considers the humanity of a terrorist—
a poem that prays for a sinner, like what Taha does in Revenge.

I think about Tsarnaev as a teen—
said to have been gregarious, friendly, funny.
He probably watched cartoons as a boy.

Then as a young man his brother whispered
Bomb. In cartoons an explosion singes a finger—
a wall crumbles but the hero walks away unscathed.

To calm my stitch I take deep breaths.
I'm on a beautiful lake surrounded by mountains.
I flip over and swim crawl.

I want to better understand lapses
in judgment—including my own.
I think about what it means to be human.

Weighing a December Swim

Standing at the water's edge
still wearing my cycling gear
I was feeling desire and regret—
the unflustered surface—tugging—
shimmering in the distance—
the water as inviting as a pond in summer—
except today the sun snakes wriggle and wander.

Here's what I don't like about uncertainty—
the way I quarrel with myself
to give both sides a fair shake—
and meanwhile the sunlight wanes
the clouds thicken, the slim window of chance
for a perfect photo closes down.

I always swam there and he did too
and then the big moon rose low
across from the setting sun
but clouds arrived and the moon set
before the night finished its blessing.

Then he slammed a car door on my arm
and even though I waived argument
he said love was not enough
or mentioned God or stopped swimming—
Then the phone went silent.

It was November and then May.
I still shudder at my indecision.
At least I no longer shout to the air
as I drive anymore—
Standing still at water's edge
I conduct myself with care.

Equinox Sunset

Too wind-weary to take a boat out for sunset
we amble across the thin section
of island, & the pink light filtered
through the trees, lures us west

as if the deep equinoxal tones
make music, a song only the sun knows
when summer breaks into autumn
when like the leaves cloud and sky display

shades of red, yellow. The song we had forgotten
rose through our bones & each time we turn
to leave, the glow reflected on a tree
draws us back to the sun.

Sweet Potato Harvest

For the sweet potato on the counter
sprouting roots like a medusa
dig a hole & bury it
with the rest of your dead—
one root for each enumerated grief:
father
mother
ex-girlfriend

Leaves blush.
Vines twist
& entwine
the fence
you built to fend off critters.

Irrigate all summer with a timer
so you don't have to attend
on days lean of rain
so that ants too might enjoy
a bath while you free yourself
to date & make an effort this time to draw lines
from the clouds—contrails to your new life—
like the ones your ex sketched so exquisitely on paper
& wasn't that her potato to begin with?

When you start to dig
don't be surprised when you hit stone.

Father on his Driveway

1.
Let me wake early
to take the brush down
to the end of the driveway.

Let me walk down carefully,
think about my steps,
rather than the brush.

2.
After my cataract surgery,
I can see—blue! Green!
But my ankles are thick as trees,
so I wear shoes I won't slip in.
I promised my daughter I wouldn't slip
again.

3.
The way flowering vines
wander across a scroll
of Japanese poetry,
I quiet my mind.

4.
Sears, Zemansky, and Young
is still tucked into the bookshelf
near my desk. I haven't cracked
it open since I retired. I still know
to go to Chapter 8 to review
Impulse and Momentum—
I used to teach that in my sleep.

5.
A young medical student lives around the corner.
Mornings, he drives by my house
on his way to the hospital.
We've never met.

6.
In my 80th year I lost my wife.
No I didn't lose her,
she expired in my arms.

7.
A 50-year-old woman comes home
and tells her husband, *The doctor told me
I had the hips of a 30 year old*. Her husband asks,
Did he say anything about your 50-year-old ass?
No, she says, *He didn't say a thing about you.*
I told that to my daughter and she laughed.

8.
On my forehead—a bandage—
my badge of honor,
taped there by the medical student
who passed by when I rolled
down the driveway.

9.
My own forgetfulness
came to me this morning
when I met the stubborn vine
at the foot of the driveway—
One more I thought *for the brush can*
but I forgot to brace myself
when I tugged and tugged, until
I won, so as it broke free—
my momentum—
I fell back, rolled down the concrete,
and when I reached bottom,
all bloodied, I thought of my wife,
who used to tend to our yard,
my wife, who used to take out the brush.

First Shots

Keep it on AUTO I say
snapping two photos of my husband
and then explain how to review them.

I hand over the Olympus—
his first digital—as he has to learn.
He's going to China—a three-week trek—

and wants to share his journey
with me in images when he comes back.
He's done this kind of trekking before—Nepal, Peru, Bosnia.

He used to leave the photography
to the *experts*—return with old low-res postcards
and cheap T-shirts—lots of them.

Sometimes he'd bring back a rug
sometimes a necklace for me.
It's all too much—too much stuff

and it weighs on me especially today—
I feel so tired. I think it's the Lyme
come back and I just want to sit.

But I say Look, here's the power button—
where it says On/Off. And here's the zoom.
If you keep it on AUTO

you won't have to worry about the light,
the speed. He can't stop thinking
about the old Leica, his light meter

and says I'll study the manual
as he takes the camera from my hand
to form his first shots.

I'm wearing my turquoise print fleece—
a favorite we picked out in New Mexico—
my hair color, a wound-down gray

I can't be bothered to change.
At his command—*Hold still*
I look into the camera.

I smile with my lips closed.
I think how nice it will be
when he goes.

Dedication

When I tackle a pile of dusty papers
sort the recycling from the mementos
it's not the scraps of writing I hope
to cull into drafts—call my own again—
that remind me of you—it's when I throw
things away   I think of the way you clean
while you plan for the small shelf—before born—
we don't know we'll love—first you measure then
drill and cleat and screw   leave room for wires
to snake through from behind   to power
up the phones and tablets—even flashlights—
and when you're done how you bowl up each rug—
take it out and shake   then sweep away the bits
of sawdust   that remain.

Voodoo

In the dream you mentioned you wanted to search online—
that is, use *OK Cupid*, match.com and the like—
not to meet a new mate, but rather to collaborate.

My throat tightens. My face yellows.

I wonder if a computer would match us up now
if I submitted my own profile—
what would I say about myself?

When dancing, knows how to refrain from taking the lead,
but dances to her own beat?

Would we surely match
if, like in a Voodoo prayer,
I include a photo of you
along with mine?

Instead, on one of those not-looking-to-date sites
I create a *you* profile—compose a lament.
I select someone—a beautiful woman with a high voice

like mine to sing along. I sing your part as a bass.
I play it for you—we sound beautiful together.
Yes, you say, *maybe this is what I want.*

Leonard Cohen Argues

Ain't no Cure for Love, lust, longing, loneliness
Bird on a Wire can't cool contention
Night Comes On, a seething no breeze would bless
I'm your Man, don't buck convention
In my Secret Life we never raise a ruckus,
never fight, *That's No Way to Say Good-bye*
just sleep tight, *Everybody Knows*, unless you hush the shouts
Anthem—start again, sip the stillness, sigh
the tears, lie lucid, *Waiting for the Miracle* that turns us
inside out. *Hallelujah*
Take this Longing, Take this Waltz
and 1-2-3, 1-2-3 whenever we wrangle
Love, Itself crumbles walls
Dance … to the End of Love—dance, dally, dangle

www.ingramcontent.com/pod-product-compliance
Lightning Source LLC
LaVergne TN
LVHW041557070426
835507LV00011B/1137